What I Want You To Know

By

Shantel Rose

Isaiah 55:11

So shall My word be that goes forth from My mouth; it shall not return to Me void. But it shall accomplish what I please, And it shall prosper in the thing for which I sent it.

Poetry

What I Want You To Know

Shantel Rose

Contents

Poetry

Introduction

The statement has been phrased — to question, to challenge, to discuss, what it is that we know. What it is that we see and observe. Symptoms of racism, oppression, and everything that comes with being black passed down from one generation to the next. Do we question and ask ourselves what it is that we see, or do not see, but it seems to suffocate us with its invisible grasp. A hold that is fierce and unrelenting in its pursuit to forever strangle and to keep us docile. "What I Want You To Know" is not only phrased for you, its for us, for us all, to contemplate and to address from both perspectives. To heal, to grow, to acknowledge, to change. It is for you to come to your own understanding. It is for you to challenge and attest what you see. Unrelenting truth, unrelenting pursuit, unrelenting fear, unrelenting courage, unrelenting love. This is what I want you to know.

Swept Under The Rug

Swept under the rug
Its all been swept under the rug
The truth
The lies
The torture
The shame
The violence
The hate
Slavery
Genocide
Segregation
Mass incarceration
Its all been swept under the rug
No acknowledgement
No accountability
No apologies
No empathy
Swept under the rug
As if it never happened
Swept under the rug
To forget
Murder
Rape
Torture
Lynching
Assimilation
Languages destroyed
Cultures destroyed
Land taken
People taken
Resources taken
Its all been swept under the rug
With no acknowledgement
To forget

It Is All By Design

It is all by design
Slavery is by design
Segregation is by design
Mass incarceration is by design
Poverty is by design
The system is by design
This society is by design
It didn't just happen
Things and orders were put into place for it to be and re-
main so
It is all by design
The ghettos are by design
The failed school systems are by design
The gentrification is by design
It is all by design
To oppress and to confine you within the state of which
they want you to live
To oppress and confine you to be and remain nothing
This country is by design
The laws are by design
It is all by design

It's Sad What's Been Done To You

It's sad what's been done to you
There's no unity among the people
Disconnected
Separated
Put against each other
Doing their bidding…. of you killing each other
You are not whole
You are now the mass segregation of their colonization
You do not have control of your land
Of what's beneath your feet
Of your history that's been distorted and rewritten right be-
fore your eyes
You are not whole
It's sad what's been done to you
Looked upon with pity
Looked upon with loathing
For, you have remained in the cycle of where they want
you to be
Held down and held back
You have been pillaged
The people, the land, the resources
You are being pillaged
I know what I want from you
To stand up and have unity of our people throughout the
world
And for us to have pride in you where ever we are
It's sad what's been done to you
Africa
The Land of Blacks
It's sad what's been done to you

We Were Never Savages

We Were Never Savages
A term used to tarnish our image
From the time of entrapment until now
Savages
Lowly creatures
Uneducated
Uncivilized
Not trained
Not developed
Not human
An image that is tarnished
Dismantled
For the betterment of their cause
Their cause to keep us in bondage to be sold into slavery
Savages were not taken from the land of Africa
People…
People were taken from the land of Africa
People were traded and sold into slavery
People were abused and mistreated
People were harmed and discarded
People were tortured
People were murdered
People were raped
Not savages
People
African People
Black people
We were never savages
Today, I see and know who the real savage is….
The savage is the one who committed all these atrocities
For — that is inhumane and uncivilized

Where Did Your Nigger Come From?

Where did your nigger come from?
Because it wasn't me
It wasn't my mother
It wasn't my father
It wasn't my grandmother
It wasn't my ancestors
We — are human beings
Human beings
Not a nigger
So, where did your nigger come from?
Why do you find the need to have a nigger?
Does your fictional nigger make you feel better
Does your fictional nigger make you feel superior
Was your fictional nigger created to worship you
I am not your nigger
So, what is it about you that wants to confine me to be
something that I am not
What is it about you that makes you want to have a nig-
ger?
A nigger to feel better than
A nigger to oppress
A nigger to control
A nigger to hurt
Where did your nigger come from?
Because it wasn't me

You Created Something To Hate

You created something to hate
You created something to confine into bondage
You created something to torture
You created something to oppress
You created something to feel better about yourselves
You created something to profit from
You created something to hurt
You created something to control
You created something to murder
It seems to me that the issue lies with you

I Do Not Envy Them Of Their Blood Money

I do not envy them of their blood money
For, I know what it took to acquire that
Rape, torture, murder, and unimaginable inhumane treat-
ment
We have let them strip us bare
Bare of our dignity
Of our pride
Of our self respect
Bare, for the love of our race and many cultures within
I do not envy them of their blood money
For, I know my people will prosper, and begin to build and
take back what's been stolen
Our land
Our culture
Our history
Our people
Our pride
Our self respect
I do not envy them of their blood money
Nor, do I feel inferior
For how can I feel inferior to such evil and hate — knowing
what they've done and suppressed — I no longer feel infe-
rior to such atrocities
For, I see the beauty in my people
I see the beauty in their resilience
I see the beauty in our cultures
I see the beauty when we dance
I see the beauty when we sing
I do not envy them of their blood money

Black Wall Street Massacre

Black wall street massacre
What do you know of this?
Along with everything else, it is buried and not known to
most
Another continuous representation of their destruction and
hatred
A prosperous time for black people
A prosperous community
A prosperous environment
Burned down in one night
Years of hard work and labor to achieve and attain wealth
Destroyed in one night
A planned massacre carried out in one night
A massacre of wealth
A massacre of families
A massacre of black people — caged in and destroyed in
one night
Businesses destroyed
Homes destroyed
Lives destroyed
Lives taken
Families destroyed
An overnight massacre
Carried out by hatred and jealousy
Carried out by resentment
Bombs deployed on this community to wipeout everything
they worked for
Bombs deployed on this community to erase their
achievements
Bombs deployed to kill
What do you know of this?
This planned overnight massacre
Since then no justice has been served
Since then no restitution has been given

Like our history it has been erased and buried to be forgotten

Viral Execution

Viral execution
Is what we are seeing today
We have been executed for centuries
With no remorse
With no justice
Bodies purposely left in the streets — perpetuated to be nothing
Left in the streets as filth
Left in the streets on display
Left in the streets as a clear message to us
Left in the streets as a warning to us
Left in the streets to intimidate
Left in the streets to deviate us from our cause and fight
Viral public executions — is what we are seeing today
Do not be afraid
For, this exposes them to be what we know they already are

What Evil Looks like

What evil looks like
There is such a thing that can be visualize
It is visualized through history
Through genocide
Through segregation
Through lynching
Through Emmitt Till
Through the scarred backs of slaves from lashes
Through the gathering festivities of watching and celebrating a lynching
Through the breading farms of people
Through the buck breaking farms of people
Through slavery
This is what evil looks like
There is no other way to define what we see and has been done
It reigned free for centuries
Basked in its glorious deeds
Relish their rights to murder
Relish their rights to degrade
Relish their rights to justify these acts as if they were humane
Relish their rights to justify…
This is what evil looks like

When We Say Black Power

When we say black power
It does not mean we hate anything other than
It is taking back
Love
It is taking back
Pride
Respect
Culture
When we say black power
You get scared because you know what your….
White power means to us and everyone else
White power has signified
Lynching
Murder
Hate
Evil
Torture
So do not equate yourselves to us when we say black
power
For we are taking back
Love
History
Do not equate yourselves to us with such hatred and evil
Black power means love
So…
When we say black power
It does not mean we hate anything other than
However….
When you say white power
We know
We see
And understand the stench that comes with that
So please

Do not equate what your meaning has been and continues
to be
With our meaning of love and taking back
What has been lost and uprooted throughout centuries
Do not equate your meaning with ours

We Need To Organize

We need to organize — for today, and tomorrow
Organize to attain prominence
Organize to be better equip for now and for the future
Consistently, we have been divided, letting personal views
affect the advancement of our people
Consistently, we have been put against each other imple-
menting our own demise
Ignorant of our actions
An accomplice to the genocide of our people
Aiding those that wish to harm us
No longer can we remain in this endless cycle
Field negroes vs house negroes
Educated negroes vs uneducated negroes
Light skin vs dark skin
We need to come together as one — to prosper and live
without restraints
We need to come together to help and teach each other
We need to come together to support each other
We need to come together
No longer can we remain unorganized for the pursuit
No longer
We have been unorganized for centuries
Enough time has been put in
Enough time has been wasted
More than enough time

The Book Of Lies

The book of lies
Are still being used and taught today in schools
Filled with lies, skewed stories, masquerading as truth
Lies specifically told and chosen to persuade your mentali-
ty
Lies made up to corroborate that our history was and is
nothing
Lies demeaning and damaging of our image
I went through my own process of studying — since my
inauguration within the american school system
A school system where African American history is taught
as an elective
A school system that erases anything that does not fit in
with its agenda
The book of lies
Still resides on the shelves in elementary schools
Still resides on the shelves in colleges and universities
Still resides in libraries— for rental or purchase
Very powerful book that is vehemently holding onto its
power
Holding on to the minds that have already succumbed to
their teaching
Holding on to its oppression
Holding on its agenda
Do not underestimate the power of this book
For, it is still being held up as truth

Read

Read
For, it is no longer illegal for us to do so
Read
The laws have changed
Read about history, philosophy, literature, poetry,
Read about Marcus Garvey
Read about James Baldwin
Read about Malcolm X
Read about the people that have fought for their rights
Read to discover your history and define your own journey
Read
For — the books are no longer separated between whites
and blacks
There are no more categories for what we can and cannot
read
There are no more categories for what we are allowed to
read
So read
We no longer have to be fearful in educating ourselves
We no longer have to be fearful being caught with a book
in our hands
We no longer have to be fearful
The times have changed
Slightly....
But, they have changed
Read to attain knowledge and wisdom
Read to see and understand different perspectives
In this matter we need to be accountable, we can no
longer sit by and remain ignorant
In this matter it is unacceptable to remain ignorant
In this matter we have to educate future generations to
come
So read

What Do You Know Outside Of What Has Been Taught To You?

What do you know outside of what has been taught to you?
Do you know your true history
Do you know the skewed version of your history
Do you consider to travel and see the world
Do you think of Africa and what you could contribute
Do you know why you are oppressed
Do you know why you are rejected
Do you know why you are resented
Do you know why you are hated
Do you know why you are held down
Do you seek information to gain knowledge
What do you know outside of what has been taught to you?
Do you know how the rest of the world views you
Do you think they are laughing with or at you
Do you think they look upon you with respect
Do you think about what has been taught to you
Do you only see your predicament
Do you only accept your predicament
What do you know outside of what has been taught to you?
What do you really know?

Have We Stopped To Think

Have we stopped to think
Have we stopped to live
Going through daily life with your heads down....
Focused on the next job
Focused on the next bill
Car payment
Light payment
Mortgage payment
Insurance payment
Have we stopped to live and enjoy
Do we consider that it's possible to live and enjoy life
Have we stopped to look
Look at the sky
Look at a flower
Enjoy the gift of rain, snow — magical elements
Have we traveled to see the world or the next neighbor-
hood
Have you woken in the morning, to just enjoy the morning
Sat in the evening to relax, look out your window and think
Have we stopped to think about the next generation in line
What has been accomplished for them to prosper
What has been accomplished for them to live freely
What can we do to ensure that their struggle will be a little
less harder
Have we stopped to consider
Consider their lives, our lives
Consider our place in society
Consider our place in history
Consider our place at their feet
Have we stopped to think
Acknowledge what has been done
Do we seek peace
Peace of mind
Peace in being
Peace to love   24

Peace to live
Peace to care
What do we seek

We See The Truth Of Our Circumstances Everyday

We see the truth of our circumstances everyday
The lies told
The laws made to keep us locked down and docile
We see what's been done to the community
We see what's been done to the black family
We've been shut out
Shut out from living
Their foot on our necks in place to make them feel better
about themselves
We see the truth
We know the truth
Yet, we remain locked down and docile
We see the truth
But are scared to challenge and attest
We see the truth
We know the truth
Today is time to take action
Remove their foot from your neck

It Seems To Me That We Accept These Terms Without Consideration

It seems to me that we accept these terms without consideration
Nigger
Nigga
Negroes
An evolution of adjustments to a name instrumented to oppress us
Hyper predators
Super predators
Animalistic branding to subject us to nothing
An image that is torn away and distorted
An image that is degraded
It seems to me that we accept these terms without consideration
We accept them in our actions
We accept them in our languages
We accept them in our living
Yet, do we really understand what it is that we are subjecting ourselves to
Do we understand the evolution of these names
Thugs
Gang bangers
Do we know the root of these titles
Do we know why they came about from our end
Do we know why we live within these labels
Black women
Black men
Black children
Names and images distorted to keep you in chains
Names and images distorted to keep you in place
Names and images distorted to show the world that they are better off without us

Names and images distorted to show the world we are
nothing, and will continue to mean nothing
And it seems to me that we accept these terms

To Bleach Or Not To Bleach

To bleach or not to bleach
Tells me your state of mind
To bleach
Shows me your self hatred — to be anything other than
black
To bleach
Shows your resentment for the color of your skin
To bleach
Shows how mentally damaged we are — to try to disasso-
ciate with being black
To bleach
Shows how much we still hurt
To bleach
Gives them the power that they are better than us — for
here we are trying to lighten our skins
To bleach
Reveals yet another trauma of what we continue to face
To bleach
Tells me that you are not proud to be black
Think about what the act of bleaching symbolizes
Think about the message that is being spread with such an
act
Think about why you feel the need to lighten your skin
Think about why you feel light skin will make you better
Think about why you think light skin will make you better
than
Think about why you rigorously try to strip away your pig-
ment
To bleach
Profits from your lack of low self esteem
To bleach
Continues the idea of what they perpetuate
So, what is your reason for bleaching?
Let's start there to repair mentally and from within our
hearts   29

This skin

This skin
Should not be a burden to you or to anyone
It is not a problem
It is not a curse
It should not be resented
It should not be feared
This skin is beautiful
Beautiful dark
Beautiful brown
Beautiful caramel
All the different shades and variations are beautiful
Each tone is unique
Each touch is uniquely soft
This skin
I am proud of
This skin
I treat with care
This skin
I love
This skin — is my armor

What Do You Tend To?

What do you tend to?
Is it love
Is it money
Is it materialist things
Is it your family
Is it your enemy
Is it your spirit
Is it your conscious
Is it humanity
Is it hate
Is it your career
Is it your pride
Is it your shame
Is it your guilt
Is it your accomplishments
Is it your faults
Is it your wisdom
Is it your knowledge
Is it your perseverance
Is it you
What do you tend to?

If You Had Self Respect You Would Dress Differently

If you had self respect you would dress differently
Walk differently
Carry yourself differently
Talk differently
If you had self respect, you would not dress without care
If you had self respect, you would treat each other with care
And love
And tenderness
With pride
With worth
With value
If you had self worth — then I would have no need to inquire and impose

Walk Differently And See What Happens

Walk differently and see what happens
Walk with pride
Walk with respect
Walk with care
And you will see what happens
Walk to show that you are somebody
Not the problems of what you've been dealt with
Walk to show that you care about your state of being
Walk differently and see what happens
Walk with confidence
Walk with love
Walk in union
And you will see what will happen
Walk with ease
Walk with acknowledgement
Walk with awareness
Walk with understanding
And you will see what happens
Walk with comfort
Walk with a smile
Walk with your head held high
And you will see what will happen

Do We Not Have Value For Our Lives Anymore?

Do we not have value for our lives anymore?
The way we treat each other is despicable
The fight
The hate
The disrespect
I see no unity
I see no care
I see no help
I see no love
I see no respect
I see no pride
Where is the value?
To walk without respect —people will treat you with no respect
To walk without care — none will be extended to you
Do you not know that you deserve better than what's been extended to you
The change has to start with you and within
The change has to start with the pursuit for true knowledge
The change has to start with the communities
I am tired of seeing you live in broken homes
I am tired of seeing you live as filth
I am tired of seeing you live in fear
I am tired of seeing you live in complacency
I am tired of seeing you live with inferiority
Where is the value?
Where is the pride?
Where is the respect?
Where is the care?
Where is the love?
Where is the strength?
Where is the fight?

Do You Know Your Purpose?

Do you know your purpose?
What is it that you see for you life
Something so innate within you to change this world in the
smallest or the largest ways possible
What are you driven to do with your life?
Is it waiting on the corner
Is it striving for an education
is it politics
Is it opening your own business
Is it fighting against poverty
Is it fighting against oppression
Is it waiting to buy a 40 ounce beer to sit and waste your
day away
Is it selling dope
Is it selling yourself
Do you know your purpose?
Is it being a lawyer
Is it being an engineer
Is it being an inventor
Is it being a crackhead
Is it being a hustler
Is it being a doctor
Is it being an advocate
Is it writing
Is it singing
Is it dancing
What is it that you see for your life?
Are you certain about the ways and how you spend your
days
Are you certain about what you can contribute for now and
the next generation
What were you meant to do?
Have you considered this.....

When Will You Stop Waiting?

When will you stop waiting?
Waiting for someone to fix your predicament
Waiting for someone to tell your true history
Waiting to be acceptable
Waiting to be respected
Waiting for permission to live
Waiting for a handout
Waiting to build and rebuild
Waiting around in a perpetual state of unrest
Waiting around in disarray
Waiting around in shame
Waiting around for opportunities
When will you stop waiting?
I'm tired of waiting
Aren't you?

To Wait For Them Is To Wait In Poverty And Disarray

To wait for them is to wait in poverty and disarray
Do we not see this?
To wait for them to build our communities is absurd
To wait for them to uplift you is absurd
To wait for equality to be handed out is absurd
To wait for justice to be given is absurd
To wait for all the wrongs to be righted is absurd
For only you can change your circumstances
Only you can demand respect
Only you can build the communities and start to properly
educate the next generation
Only you can stand face to face with history
When will we understand that it starts with us
We have to fix and rebuild our situation and our own image
We have to fix and fight against the broken system
Its in our hands
And our hands only to fight for the freedom to live
To wait for them — is a death sentence within its own right

Stop Walking Around Being Exactly What They Reduced You To Be

Stop walking around being exactly what they reduced you
to be
Take notice of their indignant when you walk any other way
Take notice of what's around you
Take notice
Stop perpetuating their stereotypes of what they want you
to be
Nothing
Useless
Self loathing
Please stop
Please…
It hurts to see how we tear each other down
It hurts to see the self hatred pouring from your pours
It hurts to see the state of disarray
Stop walking around being exactly what they reduced you
to be
Please stop…

I Used To Think We Were Nothing

I used to think we were nothing
That black wasn't beautiful
That we had no history
That we had no achievements
The hate and lies poured down my throat
Seeped its way into my mind
Into my heart
I used to think we were nothing
Spoon fed hate of race, with a dash of no self respect
Took my fill and succumbed to the symptoms that over
took me
Took my fill of their delusion as to what it means to be
black
Took my fill…
Of dirt
Of garbage
Of vile superiority complex
Took my fill of what this country continues to perpetuate
I used to think we were nothing
How sad and low my mentality was
How ashamed I am of myself for thinking that
How ashamed I am…
But herein lies the beauty of growth, of self respect, of
pride
Of love in being black
Of knowledge
Of history
Of culture
Today, I see and know the beauty of what it means to be
black through my own eyes
Their spoon is no longer at my mouth
Their vile words and hate no longer seeps into…
Into my mind
Into my heart
For, I see their daily agenda   39

Now standing face to face with my daily agenda
Of truth
Of what I used to think
Ready to combat and dispel their lies

I Used To Think How Weak We Were

I used to think how weak we were
As a people
As a race
As a community
You were weak in my eyes
Succumbing to hate
Succumbing to bondage
Succumbing to segregation
Succumbing to slavery
Succumbing to everything that was tossed your way
You were weak in my eyes
Weak for taking their treatment
Weak for being passive
Weak for not standing up
Weak…
But now I think about your perseverance
Now I think about how strong you were to live through such
atrocities
Now I think about how incredibly strong you were
To bare
To fight
Your resilience through it all is astounding
For, I could not see myself living in those times
It is inconceivable to me
Your strength is powerful
Your love is everlasting

I Used To Think It Was A Bad Thing To Refer To Each Other As Brothas And Sistahs

I used to think it was a bad thing to refer to each other as
brothas and sistahs
Now, I see the beauty in that and the depth of love we
have in our souls for each other
Love that surpasses blood link
And weaves deeper through time and eternity
A connection that stays and lingers, with each passing
moments of understanding, laughter, and pain
My brothas
My sistahs
I stand with you through this time of uplifting and support-
ing each other
I stand with you through this time of rediscovering our
beauty and our history
I stand with you now and through eternity

Their Love Is Everlasting

Their love is everlasting
The pain
The humiliation
The love
Their sacrifice — is like no other
Tears
Sweat
Blood
Grief
Sorrow
These elements were given for us to have a better life
These elements were given for our tomorrows
These elements were given for us to prosper
Some were strong
Some were broken
Some saw beyond their meager existence
Some only saw the limit of tomorrow
Some fought
Some were frightened
Others were brave
Others showed courage
Through it all, it was for our betterment — despite their
displacement
It was for our betterment
Their love is everlasting
They are — our Ancestors

Pretending It Never Happened — Won't Heal The Wound

Pretending it never happened — won't heal the wound
It seems that were are in a society that forever wants to
pretend and disregard the suffering that black people went
through
It seems that it needs to be this thing to quickly cover up
and forget
Pretending that evils acts were never committed, does not
erase the lives that were taken and the trauma that has
been endured
Pretending or disassociating the centuries of torture does
not make the pain go away
So, why are we pretending that these things never hap-
pened?
Pretending slavey never happened
Pretending that a race of people were not kidnapped
Pretending racism is not alive and well
Pretending as if years of trauma is still not being dealt with
Pretending that people and lives weren't displaced
Pretending segregation never happened
Pretending mass incarceration is not happening
It seems that others are allowed to never forget — with the
exception of us
It seems that we need to quickly get over what has been
done — as if people are still not dealing with the symptoms
of what has been done
Symptoms that we see today within the youths
Symptoms that we see today in adults
Symptoms that we see today in the communities
Symptoms that we still see today of self hatred
Symptoms that we still see today of lack of regard for one-
self
Today, what we see are the symptoms of what has been
done and continues to be perpetuated

Today, we still see the symptoms of displaced people trying to make sense of where they are and what is their purpose
Today, we still see the symptoms of the disconnection with the motherland and how that plays into finding out who you are as an individual and collective history
We see all these symptoms today — yet we disregard them and the people as just another low life that has no value
Another low life that is going nowhere
Another low life that does not contribute to society
Another low life that is taking up space
We see the symptoms of it all — yet we pretend as if they are not there
We see the symptoms of it all — yet we disregard the struggle within
We see the symptoms of it all — yet this society continues to fabricate other blames for the predicament of black people in this country
We see the symptoms of it all
So, why are we pretending that these things never happened?

Today We Scream From Our Lungs

Today we scream from our lungs
"Black Lives Matters"!!
Shouting for justice
Shouting for peace
Shouting for us
Shouting for love
Shouting to be heard
"Black Lives Matters"!!
Shouting against racism
Shouting against oppression
Shouting for the future
Today we scream from our lungs
Remember
Our ancestors screamed as well
They sang spirituals
They sang the gospel
They praised the lord
Today
We need more than screaming
We need more than singing
We need action
To rebuild and acquire for us and the next generation to
come
We need action
To make our lives better
We need action
Reach out to our youth to let them know they matter
Their lives and their future matters
We need action for organization
Today we scream from our lungs
"Black Lives Matters"!!
To who or whom are you screaming to?
Are we saying it to them or for us?

Life Will Break You — At The Least It Will Bend You

Life will break you — at the least it will bend you
The journey is a never ending process in discovering who you are and what is your purpose in life
It will shape and mold you to be the person who you really are — whether it may be good or bad
It will test your virtues or lack thereof
It will challenge you; in which you will rise or fall
Never ending rises
Never ending fallings — to pursue who you are
Yet, when it bends you, know that it is doing what it ought to do — for you to adjust and be stronger
When it bends you — admit your state of being to address what it is that was bent
When it breaks you — know that it was for a change
When it breaks you — do no remain lost and broken, dig deeper to find the strength to stand up again while you quiver
When it breaks you — address why you were broken
When it breaks you — find the pieces that has been scattered to build a stronger you
Life is ever changing
We are ever changing
This is inevitable
Each year we continue to bend
Each year we continue to break
Stand face to face with who you are and could be
Stand and fight
To hide and cower away does no good
To hide will perpetually keep you bent
To hide will perpetually keep you broken
So cry if you need to
Scream if you need to

No matter what your circumstances are — do not remain unfinished in your pursuit

There's No Need To Stay Sitting On The Floor While They Walk Past You

There's no need to stay sitting on the floor while they walk
past you
There's no need to stay sitting on the floor while life passes
by you
There's no need to stay sitting on the floor accepting
scraps of handouts
There's no need to stay sitting on the floor feeling less than
There's no need to stay sitting on the floor being looked
upon with pity
There's no need to stay sitting on the floor as trash to be
tossed out
There is no need
There's no need to stay sitting on the floor while injustice is
being done
There's no need to stay sitting on the floor being what
they've told you to be
There is no need
Rise
Stand
Learn
Gain
Prosper
Fight
Live
Be free
There's no need to wait around for them to accept you
There's no need to wait for them to look at you differently
There's no need to wait for their allowances
There is no need
Organize
Unite
Celebrate
Teach

There's no need to stay sitting on the floor while they walk past you

There's No Reason Why The Communities Should Look The Way They Do

There's no reason why the communities should look the way they do
Dumps
Rejected
Not cared for
Let's sweep together
Let's clean together
Let's eat together
Let's rebuild together
We cannot sit around waiting for them to lift us up and to give us a hand
The system itself contributed to state of the communities looking the way they do
They....
Have been keeping us in this perpetual state
We have allowed them to keep us in this perpetual state
How can we each contribute to make things better
How can we uplift and build for future generations to build up
What have we done
What is being done
There's no reason why the communities should look the way they do
Deteriorated
Unclean
Broken
Do we not see that this is a representation of us and the circumstances that we are in
Do we not see that we are better than this
Do we not see that we deserve more
We are all capable with many different talents to contribute and rebuild
Artists
Plumbers

Construction workers
Teachers
Sales associates
Managers
Mechanics
Nurses
Accountants
lawyers
Business Owners
Engineers
Writers
We all need to come together
For....
There's no reason why the communities should look the
way they do

Wake Up! — Sometimes It Seems That I Am Walking Amongst Lost Souls

Wake up! — sometimes it seems that I am walking
amongst lost souls
Head slumped
Shoulders bent
Exhausted from the ins and outs of the job
Reeking with depression
Worn out by the demands of society
Lost souls
Worn out — no identity
Lost souls
Distracted from your purpose in life
Wake up!

I Am Falling In Love With Life

I am falling in love with life
I appreciate the struggle
The risk
The hurt
The pain
The laughter
The choices
The seasons
I see things differently
I notice the clouds
The smell of fresh rain
The details of a flower; all so beautifully design
The texture of a leaf
The magic of touch
The beauty of a kiss
The butterflies of love
The tremble of apprehension
The grace of a winds touch
I am falling in love with life
I see me differently
I understand love differently
I feel things more deeply
The love
The pain
The disappointment
The triumph
The rejection
The perseverance
I am falling deeper in love with the leaf
I am falling deeper in love with music
I am falling deeper in love with poetry
I am falling deeper in love with writing
I am falling deeper in love with discovering me
I am falling deeper in love with each moments of my life
The growth   54

The resilience
The betterment of myself
Maybe we're both falling in love with each other

I Want You To Live And Be Free

I want you to live and be free
I want you to live and feel free
I want you to live without confines
I want you to live
If it is not in this country then seek elsewhere
I want you to work smart and aspire to anything you want to be
I want you to work smart
I want you to truly live and explore
I want you to travel and see many different perspectives
I want you to leave that 5 block radius
I want you to leave the cycle
I want you to see that there is so much more to life
We were not put on this earth to be that thing no one wants to deal with
We were not put on this earth to live shamefully
We were not put on this earth to live by someone else's rules
We have the right to choose how we live
We have the right to be free
We have the right to live free — we do not need to ask permission
I want you to address your mentality
I want you to address your trauma
I want so much for you
For me
For us
I want you to live and be free
I want you to live and feel free
I want you to live
Stop existing, for the sake of just existing and getting by

What I Want You To Know

What I want you to know
Is that you are strong
You are beautiful
You are resilient
You are smart
You are talented
You are somebody
You are gifted
You were never meant to be or remain nothing

Thank you for your support in reading and
sharing this message.

Shantel Rose

What I Want You To Know

Reach out to discuss, your comments, thoughts, ideas, and how you felt about the message.

shantelrose.com

rise@shantelrose.com

Instagram @shantelrose_

Amazon.com

40753816R00035

Made in the USA
Middletown, DE
22 February 2017